Teaching Story Elements With Favorite Books

Creative and Engaging Activities to Explore Character, Plot, Setting, and Theme—That Work With ANY Book!

BY ELLEN TARLOW

SCHOLASTIC
PROFESSIONAL BOOKS

NEW YORK • TORONTO • LONDON • AUCKLAND • SYDNEY

Many of the ideas in this book came out of discussions with teachers, children's literature specialists, and friends. Particularly helpful were: Frances Storey, Eileen Rush and Joan Sokotch of the Town School Reading Department in New York City, and Kit Harrison of the Camden/Rockland Elementary School in Maine. I would also like to thank Deborah Schecter, my editor at Scholastic, for her insightful suggestions and care; and Terry Cooper for helping me find and develop the topic and for making this book possible.

And special thanks to my parents, Marilyn and Bill Tarlow, for (almost) always reading me another story.

Cover and interior design by Kathy Massaro
Cover photos by Bob Lorenz
Interior illustrations by Maxie Chambliss

ISBN: 0-590-76988-X

Contents

Introduction

To explore character, plot, setting, and theme is to explore the parts of stories that children love most. Long before they make their appearance in the classroom, these story elements have captured children's imaginations. Their play, artwork, and conversation are filled with characters, events, and places found in favorite stories. Helping children structure their natural interest in story elements is the surest route to developing their understanding and love of literature.

This book was written to help you introduce story elements in a meaningful yet age-appropriate way to children in the primary grades. Every child who loves stories will be able to participate in the discussions and do the activities. More important, the lessons and activities complement the real learning goals you have for your class. Working with story elements not only helps children find more meaning in the stories they read, it also gives them tools to create their own stories.

Developing reading comprehension skills is another important reason to explore character, plot, setting, and theme. Whether your learning goals are to help students infer a character's feelings, to predict story events, or to compare and contrast real and fantasy settings, comprehension skills come directly out of story elements. The art, drama, and game-based projects in this book give children the opportunity to use these skills in a way that will spark their imaginations and develop their appreciation of literature.

A Look Inside

This book is divided into four sections: Character, Plot, Setting, and Theme. An introduction at the beginning of each section brings the learning goals for that story element into focus and offers suggestions for (1) adapting these goals to your classroom, (2) introducing the story element, and (3) extending your studies.

The individual lessons each center around a favorite classroom picture book that demonstrates a particular aspect of the story element being studied. However, the activities and other teaching ideas are all easily adaptable to a wide range of children's books. Here's what you'll find in each lesson:

Story Summary

As a brief synopsis of the book, it includes a note about the aspect of the story element that the lesson will focus on.

Learning Goals

Specific objectives identify what children will do and learn in each lesson.

Reading the Book

This section includes background and discussion ideas to help you focus on the story element before, while, and after reading the book. You'll also find ideas for charts, graphic organizers, and other ways to extend discussions and enhance learning goals.

Activity Pages

Reproducible, ready-to-use graphic organizers, charts, and other writing opportunities encourage children to reflect on the book and the story element. You'll find suggestions about how and when to use these pages most effectively. Some of these pages can also be used to help children prepare for the lesson's main activity (see below). You may wish to bind these pages together to create a Story Elements Journal for each student.

Activities

Creative and engaging hands-on projects invite children to use drama, art, writing, and even games as a way to investigate the story element. They also help children use what they have learned to innovate on the story by creating their own characters, plot, setting, or theme. The directions also include helpful tips for getting ready and for introducing the activities to students.

Each activity is adaptable to other books, allowing you to use the projects with books that are already part of your reading program. For example, the Character Treasure Chest activity that is suggested for *Miss Rumphius* (page 15) can be used with many other books whose main character exhibits strong tastes and interests. Alternate books to use with each activity are listed on the last page of each lesson.

Integrating This Book into Your Reading Program

The lessons and activities in this book can be used in a variety of ways to enhance your existing reading program. The suggestions below offer different options to help you make the best use of this book with your students.

Mini-Units on Individual Story Elements

Each of the four sections in this book can be used as a mini-unit to teach a particular story element. Allow about one to two weeks to complete each unit. Reading the section introduction will help you prepare for the unit. If you choose to do the mini-unit, following the suggested sequence is recommended. You will find that the activities and learning goals complement one another and allow children to build on learning done in the earlier lessons.

Choosing Individual Lessons

You may prefer to pick and choose individual lessons based on the activity, the book, or the learning goals. A quick glance through each section will give you an idea of which lessons best suit your needs. Everything you need to know to teach any individual lesson is contained within the lesson plan.

Choosing Activities to Use With Your Own Books

You may prefer to use the activities and other lesson ideas with your own or students' favorite books. Although the directions in each lesson refer to the book in the lesson, they are easily adaptable to a wide range of books and can be used with either the suggested alternate titles or books you feel are appropriate.

A Monthlong Story Elements Unit

You may want to set aside a month or so to do a larger Story Elements unit. Read through the introduction to each section to help you organize your unit and give you a sense of the overall learning goals and methods. Although the units can be done in any order, the sequence in which they appear (Character, Plot, Setting, and Theme) is recommended as one that helps children build on their understanding by starting with the most immediate and accessible story elements.

· C h a r a c t e r ·

For children, character can be the most immediate and accessible route into a work of literature. Characters are the heart of stories and the lifeline that connects directly to the reader. No matter how exciting the plot, how exotic the setting, or how meaningful the theme, caring about what happens to a character is often the real force that pulls us deeper into a story. Character is also the part of stories that children most easily relate to their own experiences, which makes it a particularly good place to begin their literature studies.

The books in this section introduce children to a wide range of characters: There is Frances, the hilariously mischievous badger; the sad and mysterious Crow Boy; the artistic and inspiring Miss Rumphius; and Julian, the tall-tale teller. The discussions and activities that accompany their stories focus on the following learning goals:

❋ Looking for clues to a character's personality by considering what a character does, feels, imagines, likes, and dislikes;

❋ Helping children articulate what they intuitively understand about a character through language-building activities such as dramatic play, word webs, and language-based art projects;

❋ Encouraging children to use and build on their understanding of a character through extension activities such as creating a character's treasure chest, making a character's scrapbook, or putting on a puppet play that places the character in a new situation;

❋ Helping children to "fill in" characters' unstated thoughts, feelings and motivations through activities such as "feelings" posters, monologues, and "thought balloon" storyboards.

Introducing Character

Before beginning to work with the books and activities in this section, it might be helpful to introduce children to the study of character by doing the following:

❋ Ask children to name some of their favorite book characters. Write the character's name on the left-hand column of a chart. Then ask children to tell why they like their character. Challenge them to describe the character to the class. Try to pick out the describing words or phrases—such as *funny, brave, strong, smart*—from their answers. Fill in the right-hand column of your chart with these describing words, as shown below.

Character	Why I Like This Character
Frances	She is funny.

You may want to keep this chart handy so that children can add new characters and descriptions as they read the books in this section.

Bedtime for Frances

by Russell Hoban

(HARPER TROPHY, 1960)

Will Frances ever go to bed? Not while there's milk and pie to ask for, her teddy bear to talk to, songs to make up and a scary giant to contend with. One of the best-loved characters in children's literature, Frances the badger is a distinctive personality with whom almost all children can identify. Exploring *Bedtime for Frances* will help children focus on how characters reveal themselves in everyday situations.

Learning Goals

* Describe a character by considering how she acts.

* Create a word web of character traits.

* Extend understanding of a character through character trait skits.

Before Reading the Book

Ask children to talk about the way they act and feel at bedtime. Have they ever imagined seeing scary things in the dark? What do they think about while trying to fall asleep? Do they ever make up games? sing songs? tell themselves stories? Show children the cover of *Bedtime for Frances*. Invite them to predict what Frances will do in the story and how she might avoid going to bed.

While Reading the Book

As you read, stop every few pages to ask children if they have ever acted the way Frances is acting now. Invite them to talk about how they felt when they acted in that way.

After Reading the Book

Ask children what they think of Frances. Is she a character they would like to know? Do they think she would be fun to play with? Does she remind them of anyone they know? In what way? Encourage children to focus on what makes Frances distinctive by asking how another child (or badger) might act differently at bedtime. Finally, ask how they would describe Frances to someone who hasn't read the book. What words or phrases would they choose? What examples would they use?

Create a Character Trait Web

One way to help children find words to describe characters is to create a Character Trait Web such as the one below. First, ask children to recall some of the things Frances did and said. Then elicit words or phrases that describe these actions.

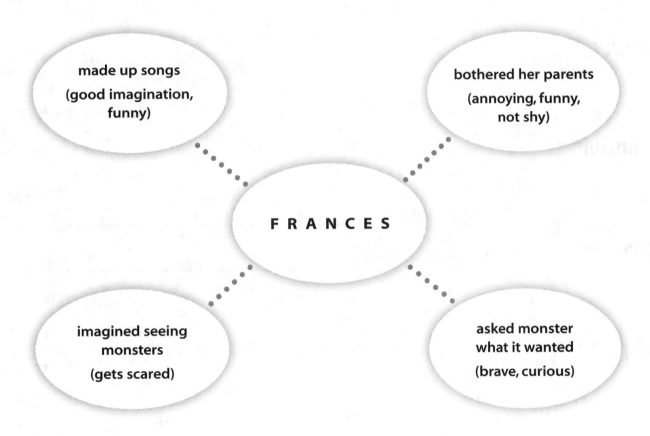

made up songs
(good imagination, funny)

bothered her parents
(annoying, funny, not shy)

FRANCES

imagined seeing
monsters
(gets scared)

asked monster
what it wanted
(brave, curious)

Activity Page

The reproducible on page 10 invites children to continue working with words that describe Frances.

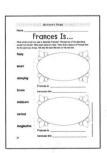

Name _____

Frances Is...

What words would you use to describe Frances? Choose two of the describing words from the list. Write each word on a line. Then draw a picture of Frances that fits the word you chose. Tell why the word fits her on the next line.

funny

smart

annoying

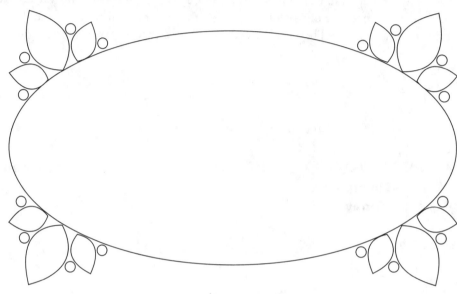

Frances is _____

because she _____.

brave

stubborn

curious

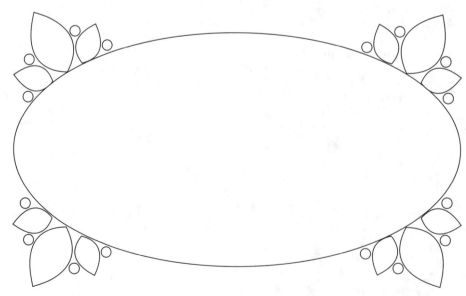

imaginative

Frances is _____

because she _____.

Teaching Story Elements With Favorite Books   Scholastic Professional Books

Character Trait Skits

Frances is an unusually colorful and animated character whom children love to imitate. This activity invites children to pull out a word from a grab bag that describes Frances and then use this personality trait to create a puppet skit based on a scene in the story.

Getting Ready

On slips of paper, write words that describe Frances from your Character Trait Web. Some words or phrases you may want to include are *funny, annoying, curious,* and *has a good imagination*. Put the slips in a paper bag. Have puppet-making materials ready, such as paper lunch bags or old socks, as well as a variety of arts-and-crafts materials such as yarn, fabric scraps, construction paper, scissors, and glue for decorating. Students will use these materials to make puppets for their skits.

Introducing the Activity

Introduce the activity by reminding children of the Character Trait Web they just made about Frances. Show the paper bag that contains the describing words and tell children what is inside. Explain that small groups will pull a word from the bag and put on a short puppet skit in which Frances acts like the word they have chosen.

Planning and Performing the Skits

1 Divide the class into groups of two or three. Let a volunteer from each group choose a describing word from the paper bag. Then help each group find a part of the book that shows Frances acting in that way. Tell students that they will make puppets to use in a puppet skit of that scene in the book.

2 Provide students with the puppet-making materials and invite them to make the characters needed for their skit. (One child can make a Frances puppet, while the others make puppets that portray the other characters in their scene.)

3 When children are ready to work on their scenes, encourage them to add new ideas. For example, if the group's word is *annoying* or *stubborn*, they may act out a scene from the book in which Frances asks her parents for something and then add to it by thinking of a new thing that Frances could bother her parents about.

4 To make a puppet stage, cover a table with a floor-length tablecloth. Invite them to crouch behind the table to act out their skits. Then ask the class to guess which describing word the skit showed.

Extension

More Frances Puppet Skits

For younger children, simply acting out the story in groups of three or four (mother, father, Frances and narrator) is good practice in understanding character. Older children may want to use their puppets to create entirely new Frances scenes. Since *Bedtime for Frances* is about an everyday situation that Frances wants to avoid, it might be helpful to think of similar situations—such as eating her dinner, going to school, taking a test, or visiting the dentist—for children to use as the basis for their new skits.

Other Books to Use with This Activity

A Bear Called Paddington by Michael Bond
(Houghton Mifflin, 1960)

Bread and Jam for Frances by Russell Hoban
(Harper Trophy, 1965)

Owen by Kevin Henkes (Greenwillow, 1993)

Miss Rumphius

by Barbara Cooney (VIKING, 1982)

When Alice Rumphius grows up, she plans to visit faraway places and live by the sea. Then her grandfather tells her there is one more thing she must do with her life: help make the world more beautiful. This poetic story follows its quietly remarkable heroine from childhood to old age, showing the various stages of her life and how she fulfills her grandfather's wish. Through reading *Miss Rumphius*, children will meet a remarkable character whose life story gives clues to the person she is inside.

Learning Goals

✳ **Explore a character by looking at how she leads her life.**

✳ **Describe a character's interests, values, and tastes.**

✳ **Express understanding of a character by creating a treasure chest that the character would keep.**

Before Reading the Book

Ask children to talk about grown-ups they admire. The grown-up can be someone they know in real life or someone that they have read or heard about. What do these people do? Would they like to be like the person they admire? In what way? Tell the class that they are going to read a book about a woman who does some special things in her life. One of the things she does is help make the world a more beautiful place. Ask: *How do you think she will do that?*

After Reading the Book

Ask the class what they think about Miss Rumphius. Is she someone that they might want to be like? Why or why not? Do they think Miss Rumphius led a good life? If so, how? Go through the book and create a word web about each new phase of Miss Rumphius's life. What words or phrases would describe a person who wants to visit faraway places? who works in a library? who loves the sea? who wants to make the world more beautiful? (Some words or phrases to include might be *adventurous, likes books, likes to do different or unusual things, likes quiet places, wants to help people, keeps her promises*.)

Activity Page

The reproducible on page 14 invites children to create their own "remarkable" life story using *Miss Rumphius* as a model.

Name _____

My Life Story

What would you like to do in your life? What does that tell about you? In the boxes below, draw and write about where you would like to live, what you would like to be, and how you would help the world. Share your work with the class.

In my life:

I want to live

_____

_____.

I want to be a

_____

_____.

I want to help the world by

_____

_____.

Teaching Story Elements With Favorite Books Scholastic Professional Books

Character Treasure Chest

Miss Rumphius is a character whose long life reveals strong interests, tastes, and values. This activity encourages children to consider what Miss Rumphius cares about as they find or make objects to put in her Treasure Chest.

Introducing the Activity

Point out that Miss Rumphius led an interesting life in which she did many things that are special and important to her. Explain that one way people express what is important to them is through the things they keep in their houses or the things they put in their "treasure chests." Invite children to share some special things they keep in their rooms or personal treasure chests.

Focus on the Character

Before doing this activity, go through the book and list the things Miss Rumphius has done and enjoys. Together, think about what each entry on your list says about what she would like to have in her Treasure Chest. Your chart might include some of the following:

Miss Rumphius Likes:	She Might Have:
• faraway places	(postcards, pictures of places, foreign-looking coins, dolls and trinkets)
• books	(stories, pictures of book characters, poems, library cards)
• the ocean	(shells, interesting rocks, fish tanks)
• flowers and nature	(pressed flowers and leaves, acorns, rocks)
• art and beautiful things	(paintings, anything beautiful or special, musical instruments)

Creating the Treasure Chest

1 Ask each child to bring a shoe box (or a larger box with a lid) to school. Have children paint the boxes or cover them with craft paper. Place the lids on the boxes.

2 To create hinged lids, have children first tape each lid to its box along one edge. Then help them slit the lid at the two corners that are taped to the box. To make a closure for the box, use a hot-glue gun (adult only) to affix a decorative button to the front of the box and a loop of ribbon to the lid.

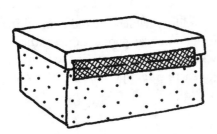 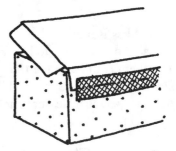

3 Set out a variety of materials—construction paper, paints, markers, spools, craft feathers, cardboard, empty milk cartons, yarn, lace, rickrack, fabric bits—for children to decorate their boxes with and to make their own versions of objects Miss Rumphius might put in her Treasure Chest. Students may also want to bring in objects they find at home or outdoors such as ribbons, doll-size tea sets, foreign coins, rocks, seashells, acorns, and leaves.

4 Have children break up into small groups to share their Treasure Chests and explain why they added different objects.

Other Books to Use with This Activity

Emily by Michale Bedard (Doubleday, 1992)

Her Majesty Aunt Essie by Amy Schwartz (Bradbury Press, 1984)

Tom by Tomie dePaola (Putnam, 1993)

Uncle Elephant by Arnold Lobel (Harper Junior, 1981)

Crow Boy

by Taro Yashima

(VIKING, 1955)

The children in the village school call him Chibi, which means "tiny boy." Chibi is always at the end of the line. In school he stares out the window and never learns anything. In the playground he is always by himself. This moving story introduces children to an unusual and sympathetic character who is different from those around him.

Learning Goals

* **Identify with a character's situation.**

* **Explore how and why a character changes in a story.**

* **Use clues from the story to fill in a character's unspoken thoughts and feelings.**

Before Reading the Book

Ask children to talk about ways they are different from other children. Do they enjoy doing things that other children don't? Do they care about things that other children don't care about? Do they look different or live in a different kind of house or family? Tell children that they are about to read a story about a boy who is different from his classmates. Show them the cover of Crow Boy. Have children predict how Crow Boy might be different and how his classmates might feel about him.

While Reading the Book

To develop children's ability to infer a character's thoughts and feelings, stop every once in a while to ask what Chibi is feeling or why he might be acting the way he is.

After Reading the Book

Ask children what they think of Chibi. How was he different than his classmates? Why do they think he was so afraid of the other children? What was Chibi good at that the other children weren't? Encourage children to discuss what Chibi is thinking or feeling inside. Ask: *What does he enjoy? What makes him sad? What makes him afraid?*

Then help children focus on some of the other important characters in *Crow Boy*. Ask what they thought about Mr. Isobe. How did he help Chibi? Do they think he was a good teacher? In what way? What did children think of Chibi's classmates? Why did they make fun of Chibi? Why did they feel bad at the last day of school? What made them change? Ask children how they might feel about Chibi if he were in their class.

Name _____

What Is Chibi Feeling?

Read each sentence from the story. Then draw a picture of Chibi that shows the sentence. In the thought bubble, write what he might be thinking or feeling.

① He was found hidden away in the dark space underneath the schoolhouse.

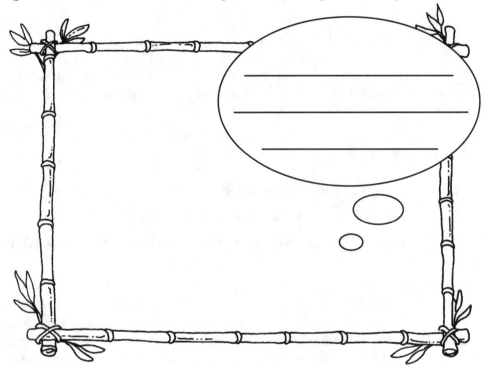

② Mr. Isobe announced that Chibi was going to imitate the voices of crows.

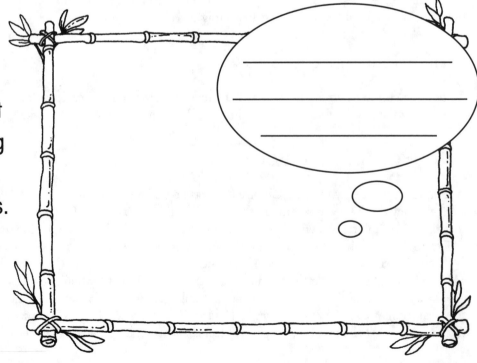

Activity Page

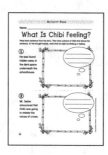

The reproducible on page 18 will encourage children to explore Crow Boy's feelings by creating thought balloons for story scenes.

Character's Feelings Poster

In *Crow Boy*, Chibi never speaks. Yet the way he acts tells a lot about what he is feeling. This activity encourages children to think about what makes Chibi happy, what makes him sad, what makes him afraid, and what makes him proud as they create a Character's Feelings Poster.

Introducing the Activity

Show children examples of posters and discuss how posters usually contain both words and pictures that work together to tell about something. Explain that they will be creating posters that show the many different ways that Chibi feels in Crow Boy. Help them brainstorm a list of feelings words that apply to Chibi. Some words to include on the list are: *happy, sad, afraid, lonely,* and *proud*. Encourage them to give examples of what makes Chibi feel that way.

Making the Poster

1 Give pairs of children a large sheet of drawing or poster paper. Then model how to create a feelings poster by drawing a large rectangle on chart paper. Title the poster "What Makes Chibi . . ." Next, divide the rectangle into four sections. On the top of one quadrant, write a feelings word such as *happy*. Ask children to suggest something that makes Chibi feel that way. For example, listening to crows, talking to Mr. Isobe, or helping out his family. Explain that in this part of their poster, students will draw one or more things that make Chibi feel happy and write a sentence or two that explains the drawing.

2 To make their posters, invite children to choose four feelings words from the class list to illustrate and write about. You may want to put out fabric, buttons, tissue paper, and other craft materials so that they can add some collage elements. Remind students to title their posters like the example on the chart paper and to organize the space on the poster to accommodate each feeling word.

19

First-Person Narrations

Older children may also want to explore Crow Boy's inner feelings by rewriting the story in the first person. Or they may want to make a "filmstrip" version of the story and show it on a homemade "projector."

- To make their projectors, provide each student with a clean, empty milk carton (pint or half-pint size). Help them cut open the bottom of the carton, then cut a 2 1/2-inch slit in each side, as shown.

- Hand out long strips of paper that are about 2 1/2 inches wide. Students can then write and illustrate their stories using speech or thought balloons to tell what Chibi is thinking and feeling.

- To view their filmstrips, have students thread the strips through the slits in the milk carton and pull the strip through the projector. Invite students to share their filmstrips with classmates.

Other Books to Use with This Activity

Lily's Purple Plastic Purse by Kevin Henkes (Greenwillow, 1996)

Stevie by John Steptoe (Harper & Row, 1969)

Sylvester and the Magic Pebble by William Steig (Little Simon, 1988)

The Stories Julian Tells

by Ann Cameron (RANDOM HOUSE, 1981)

No one tells stories quite like Julian does. And no one knows what he's going to come up with next. One of his stories might be about the catalog cats (cats that you order from a catalog), or the way eating fig leaves really helps him to grow, or it might be about his "cave-boy" teeth. This collection of easy-to-read stories introduces children to a lively first-person narrator whose active imagination gives interesting clues to the person he is inside.

Learning Goals

☀ **Explore a character by looking at the way he uses his imagination.**

☀ **Connect and build on understanding of a character by reading new episodes that reveal new facets of his personality.**

☀ **Extend understanding of a character by making a character's scrapbook.**

Before Reading the Book

Ask children what kinds of things they like to make up or imagine. Have them share some examples. What do they think their stories tell about what they enjoy and what interests them? Tell the class they are going to read about a boy who likes to tell stories. Show children the cover of the book. Have them break up into small groups to make a list of what Julian's stories might be about.

Create an Ongoing Character Map

After reading the first episode, ask children what they think of Julian. Start a One Character/Many Stories Map such as the one on page 22. Have children tell what Julian did and imagined in the first story. Then have them think of what this tells about Julian. Write down these words and phrases. After each episode you read, refer back to the map. Ask children if Julian still has some of the qualities that they originally named. Check off the qualities that still apply. Add to the list by asking children what else they learned about Julian during the new episode.

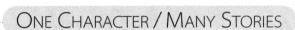

What is Julian like?

"A Pudding..."	"Catalog Cats"	"Our Garden," etc.
Funny	yes	yes
Makes things up	yes	yes
Disobeys father	yes	
Fools his brother	yes	
Nice to his brother	yes	yes
Likes sweet things		yes
Feels sorry for his mistakes	yes	
	Likes to help his father	yes
	Likes cats	
	Believes his own stories	yes
	Likes to garden	yes
	Likes quiet times	

Activity Page

After reading the stories, invite children to think of their own idea for a "Julian" story by filling in the reproducible on page 23. Have students use the back of the page if they need more room to write.

Name _____

Julian Tells Another Story

Think of your own "Julian" story. Pick one of the ideas below. Then on the book pages, write your ideas for a new story.

Pick an Idea

* a funny excuse for being late to school

* a new way to make money

* a new way to fool Huey

_____

_____

_____

_____

_____

_____

_____

_____

Character Scrapbook

Julian, the tall tale-telling, monster-loving, wish-list-making narrator of *The Stories Julian Tells*, is full of ideas and interests. One way people express and share interests is through a scrapbook. This activity asks children to imagine that they are Julian and to make a scrapbook filled with the kinds of things that Julian might like.

Introducing the Activity

Tell children that they are going to create "Julian's Scrapbook." Ask what they know about scrapbooks. Why do people keep them? What kinds of things do people put in them? What can they learn about a person from looking at their scrapbook? You may wish to develop a chart such as the following:

What a Scrapbook Might Include

* information about/pictures of interests and hobbies
* samples of things the person collects
  (leaves, baseball cards, stickers)
* ads for favorite movies, covers of favorite books
* pictures of places the person wants to go
* pictures of heroes and people the person admires
* awards the person has won, report cards, other accomplishments
* favorite drawings the person has done
* pictures of family and friends
* pictures/information about favorite animals and pets

Focus on the Character

Before beginning, invite children to think about what kinds of things they might include in Julian's scrapbook. Explain that some things can be taken right from the book. For example, they know that Julian is interested in cavemen and loves cats— so pictures and information about cats, dinosaurs, and cavemen might be part of his scrapbook.

Then tell them that they also will be making up scrapbook entries based on what they think Julian would like, using information from the stories. For example, since they know that Julian likes kite flying, what other activities might he enjoy? Since they know that Julian is very funny and loves jokes, what kinds of books and movies might he like? Julian is a bit of a trouble-maker but very interested in learning new things; what do they think his teachers would write about him on a report card? What would a boy with Julian's interests be likely to draw? You may want to go through the "What a Scrapbook Might Include" chart (see page 24) and discuss how some of the items might apply to Julian.

Constructing the Scrapbook

To make their scrapbooks, tell children to staple together several pieces of construction paper along one edge. Explain that real scrapbooks often contain objects and pictures that have been pasted to the pages. Students can do this or draw pictures instead. Have old magazines available for children to cut pictures from. Encourage them to label and write about their entries as Julian might. Then invite children to share their scrapbooks and tell why they chose to include what they did.

Other Books to Use with This Activity

Chester's Way by Kevin Henkes (Puffin Books, 1989)

Eloise by Kay Thompson (Simon & Schuster, 1969)

Ramona the Pest by Beverly Cleary (Dell, 1982)

• Plot •

To explore plot is to explore what happens in a story and why. If caring about a character helps children to become interested in a story, then a well-developed plot is what keeps them interested. Plot is perhaps the most fundamental literary element—it is what makes a story a story. And the skills and strategies developed while studying plot—such as predicting, summarizing, recognizing patterns, and relating causes to effects—are among the most essential to basic reading comprehension.

The books in this section introduce children to a wide range of plot types. There are highly structured, patterned stories such as *Why Mosquitoes Buzz in People's Ears*; predictable, problem-centered stories such as *Ming Lo Moves the Mountain*; and more complex, character-driven stories such as *Brave Irene* or *Best Friends*. Plot is the literary element that requires children to work with the greatest amount of information at the same time. Helping children organize this information is an important part of exploring plot. The following outline of simple story structure might be useful while working with the books and activities in this section:

❋ Stories typically begin by introducing characters and by presenting an initiating event that will have consequences or a problem that needs to be solved.

❋ The episodes that follow stem from the initiating event or problem. The initiating event might cause further complications. The characters might take steps to solve their problem or new facets of the original problem might be experienced.

❋ At some point the pattern is broken and a resolution occurs. The characters will either solve their problem or reach their goal, or an event will occur which alters the course of the story and brings it to a satisfying conclusion.

Dramatizations, storytelling activities, plot-centered board games, and other projects invite children to innovate on the various features of simple plots. For younger children visual representation—such as story maps or picture time lines—is an important part of the study of plot. The sample graphic organizers and charts in this section can be used with a wide range of stories.

Ming Lo Moves the Mountain

by Arnold Lobel (WILLIAM MORROW, 1982)

Living next to a mountain is causing Ming Lo no end of problems. Falling rocks make holes in his roof. His crops won't grow because sunlight never reaches his garden. And it hardly ever stops raining. When he finally visits the village wise man, he finds that there is indeed a way to move a mountain. Using traditional, repetitive folktale structure, this original story offers a clear and entertaining introduction to a simple problem/solution model of plot.

Learning Goals

* **Understand how plot is driven by a problem and a solution.**
* **Identify the characteristics of story beginnings.**
* **Create new story beginnings.**

Introducing the Book

Tell children they are going to read a story about Ming Lo, a farmer who doesn't like living next to a mountain and wants to move it. Ask them to think of reasons why he might not want to live next to a mountain. Write their ideas on the board under the heading "Problems." Then ask how he might be able to solve these problems. Write these ideas under the heading "Solutions." Invite children to find out if any of the problems and solutions they suggested appear in the story.

While Reading the Book

Before and after each visit to the wise man, ask children to predict what will happen. Is there a point at which they want to change their predictions? What new information do they have that helps them to think differently?

After Reading the Story

Point out that many stories center around a problem that needs to be solved. Ask children to describe the problem in *Ming Lo Moves the Mountain.* Then ask them to describe how Ming Lo tried to solve his problem. What do they think of the story ending? Do they think it is a "real" solution? Do they think the wise man is really wise? In what way? Invite them to refer back to the Problem/Solution chart that they made before reading the book to find out if any of their ideas were in the story.

Name _____

Wise or Unwise Solutions

Be a wise child and help Ming Lo. Draw and write about two new ways he could try to move the mountain. Your ideas can be silly, just like those in the story.

Ming Lo wanted to move the mountain. So he ...

But the mountain didn't move. Next, Ming Lo ...

And still the mountain didn't move!

Now tell how Ming Lo solved his problem.

_____

_____

Teaching Story Elements With Favorite Books Scholastic Professional Books

Activity Page

The reproducible on page 28 will help children to recognize the problem/solution structure of this story by adding new possible solutions to the original story problem. If students need more room, have them turn over the page and write on the back.

Story Beginning Grab Bags

The beginning of a story often sets the plot in motion by introducing characters, describing a problem that needs to be solved, and establishing a setting. In this activity, children will create beginnings to new stories by using information they pull out of Character, Setting, and Problem Grab Bags.

Focus on the Story Beginning

Invite a child to read the beginning of *Ming Lo Moves the Mountain*. Ask the class to raise their hands once they think the beginning is over. There may be some disagreement over where the beginning ends. You can help children by telling them that the beginning of a story often introduces the main character(s), tells about the setting (where the story takes place), and sets up a problem to be solved. Invite children to name the character in the story, to tell where the story takes place, and to describe the character's problem.

Introducing the Activity

Have three paper bags available. Label one "Characters," another "Settings," and the last "Problems." Show the paper bags to students and tell them that they are going to create beginnings of new stories using information they will make up and put into these bags.

Making the Grab Bags

1 Give children three slips of paper each. Explain that on the first slip they will write a character's name and something about that character. On the second slip they will write the name of a place and something that describes it. On the third slip they will write a story problem. It might be helpful to brainstorm kinds of characters, settings, and story problems. Since children will be putting the slips into separate bags and choosing them randomly, point out that the problems, characters, and settings don't necessarily have to go together.

2 After children have written out their characters, settings, and problems, have them place their slips of paper into the appropriate bags. Then invite children to choose one slip from each of the three bags and ask volunteers to read their slips of paper aloud. Together, think of a way to make the information into a simple story beginning. (Since the slips will be chosen randomly, many of the beginnings will be silly, yet they can still resemble traditional story beginnings in structure.) It may be helpful to read sample story beginnings from folktales or other classic books. Suggest ways that stories usually begin, such as with the phrase, *Once upon a time* or *There once was ....*

3 After children have gotten used to the process, invite them to write or tell a story beginning using the information on their paper slips. Children may want to use their story beginnings to create an entire new story.

Other Books to Use with This Activity

The City of Dragons by Laurence Yep (Scholastic, 1995)

The Mud Pony by Caryn Lee Cohen (Scholastic, 1988)

Stone Soup by Marcia Brown (Simon & Schuster, 1975)

Why Mosquitoes Buzz in People's Ears

by Verna Aardema

(DIAL, 1975)

When Mosquito tells Iguana a silly story, Iguana blocks his ears. But then Iguana doesn't hear Python's greeting. So Python fears that the animals are plotting against him. One misunderstanding leads to another until the whole jungle is in an uproar. This colorful adaptation of a traditional African tale offers an excellent example of a plot that is made up causes and effects.

Learning Goals

* Understand a plot as a series of causes and effects.

* Innovate new story events using a cause-and-effect structure.

Introducing the Book

Gather the class in a circle and invite them to play a game of "telephone." Remind children that telephone is played by whispering the same message to the child next to them. After the game is finished, ask the last child to say the message aloud. Then go around the circle and have each child tell what he or she thought the message said. Try to discover where the "faults" are. Tell the class they are about to read a story that is like the game of telephone.

While Reading the Book

Before each new episode, ask the class what the animal's action might cause to happen next. Invite children to notice how the animals misinterpret each other's actions.

After Reading the Book

Ask children what they thought of the story. How did it remind them of the game of telephone? Try to discover the story pattern by asking children how each episode leading up to the baby owl's death was the same. Encourage children to recognize that in each episode an animal reacts to another animal's actions by doing something that the following animal doesn't like or misunderstands.

Plot Picture Time Line

Help children focus on the cause-and-effect structure of the plot by making a plot picture time line. First, invite volunteers to draw or paint pictures of each animal in the story on construction paper, then cut them out. Place a roll of bulletin board paper on the floor. Then have children glue or tape the animals to the paper in the order in which they appear in the story. Invite new volunteers to write what each animal did, above or below each picture. To emphasize the causes and effects in the story, have children write the word *so* between each pair of pictures. For example, "Mosquito told a silly story" *so* "Python blocked his ears." When the time line is complete, cut it from the roll and display. Use the time line to review the plot with children. Ask them to talk about who was at fault for the baby owl's death.

Activity Page

The reproducible on page 33 will help children consider the causes and effects in the story by telling which animal they think caused the sun not to shine.

Name _____

Who Caused It?

Which animal do you think caused the sun not to shine? Was it Mosquito who started it? Or Python who scared Rabbit? Or Mother Owl who didn't do her job? Pick an animal and draw it. Then, on the lines below, write why you think that animal caused the sun not to shine.

It's all my fault! I caused the sun not to shine because

_____

_____

_____.

Freeze Frame Dramatics

Chain reaction stories such as *Why Mosquitoes Buzz in People's Ears* are excellent for acting out. This two-part activity invites children to first act out the story. The freeze-frame dramatics feature then asks the players to reenact the story, stopping after each episode so that members of the audience can suggest new actions which will have entirely new effects.

Introducing the Activity

Ask children if they have ever stopped a video while it was playing and looked at the image on the screen. Explain that this is called "freezing the frame." Tell children that they will be playing a game called "Freeze Frame." Explain that in the game, they will act out the story of *Why Mosquitoes Buzz in People's Ears.* Every once in a while, you will call out *Freeze!* This will be a cue for audience members to suggest new actions that a particular character might take.

To prepare for the activity, review the cause-and-effect structure of *Why Mosquitoes Buzz in People's Ears.* Then go through the book and invite children to suggest new reactions that each animal might have to the animal preceding it.

Playing Freeze Frame

1 Divide the class into groups of seven and assign each group member an animal in the story to play. If you like, invite children to make masks or costumes for their characters.

2 Have children act out the first part of story (until the mother owl refuses to hoot for the sun). You or another child can act as a narrator and read the story.

3 After the group has acted out the story once, have them play Freeze Frame. Tell the players to begin. Then call out *Freeze!* after Iguana listens to the Mosquito's story. Say: *Iguana doesn't want to listen to Mosquito. What could he do?* Children might suggest actions such as running away, singing loudly to himself, etc. Tell the child playing Iguana to act out one of these ideas. Then when Python appears on stage, call *Freeze!* again. Say: *Python hears Iguana singing loudly to himself. What might Python do?* Invite children to suggest new actions. Continue until all the animal players have had a turn. Repeat with other groups of children.

Other Books to Use with This Activity

The Day Jimmy's Boa Constrictor Ate the Walsh by Trina Hakes (Puffin Books, 1980)

The House That Jack Built by Jenny Stow (Dial, 1992)

If You Give a Mouse a Cookie by Laura Joffe Numeroff (Harper & Row, 1985)

The Old Ladies Who Liked Cats by Carol Greene (HarperCollins, 1991)

Brave Irene

by William Steig

(FARRAR, STRAUS & GIROUX, 1986)

On the evening of the duchess's ball, the seamstress falls ill. When her brave young daughter sets out to deliver the newly finished gown, she encounters a blizzard and other dangers on the way. Combining gentle humor, a fairy-tale setting, and an adventure-packed journey, this story introduces children to a plot in which the initiating problem leads to many new problems.

Learning Goals

✳ **Map the story by focusing on problems and solutions.**

✳ **Add to the story's middle by innovating new problems.**

✳ **Express understanding of plot by creating a story-problem board game.**

Before Reading the Book

Ask children to tell about a time they have acted bravely. As they relate their stories, help them find the "plot line." Did they act bravely in response to a problem? What was the problem? Did their actions help to solve the problem? How? Show children the book cover and tell them that they are about to read a story about a girl who journeys through a blizzard. Together, make an idea web of problems Irene might face on her journey.

While Reading the Book

As you read, have children predict how Irene will solve each problem she faces on her way to the duchess's.

After Reading the Book

Invite children to share their reactions to the story. Do they think Irene did the right thing by trying to deliver the dress? Would they have done the same thing? Can they think of another way to solve her problem? What did they think was the most exciting part of the book? What was the most difficult problem Irene faced? As you discuss the story episodes, you may want to fill in a problem/solution story map such as the one on the next page.

Main Story Problem
The duchess's dress needs to be delivered, and the mother is too sick to go.

Solution
Irene will go instead.

Next Problem
There is a blizzard.

Solution
Irene dresses very warmly.

Next Problem
It is too windy for Irene to walk.

Solution
She walks backward.

Next Problem
The wind carries away the dress box.

Solution
Irene decides to go on anyway.

Activity Page

The reproducible on page 38 invites children to add to the story's middle by creating new problems Irene could face on her journey.

Name _____

The Further Adventures of Brave Irene

During the blizzard, Brave Irene faced many problems. In the boxes below, draw and write about two new problems that could have happened on Irene's journey.

The snow was coming down so hard that Brave Irene

_____

_____ .

All of a sudden _____

and Brave Irene _____ !

Teaching Story Elements With Favorite Books   Scholastic Professional Books

Problem/Solution Board Game

The plot of *Brave Irene* centers on how Irene overcame many difficulties on her journey to the duchess's. This board game activity asks children to add to the story's middle by inventing and solving new problems that Irene could have faced on her way.

Introducing the Activity

Review with children the many problems Irene overcame on her journey. Point out that these are only a few problems a story character might face on an important journey. Then show children a board game such as Monopoly. Explain that they will be making their own board game called "On the Way to the Duchess's." Tell children that the point of the game will be to get their Irene playing piece to the duchess's. They will do this by thinking of new problems that Irene could face on her journey and writing them on Problem Cards. As they play the game, children will pick a Problem Card from the pile and think of a possible solution. Then they can move their Irene piece the number of spaces indicated on the card.

Creating the Board Game

1 Give groups of five children each a large sheet of paper or cardboard for making a game board. Point out that the game board should have at least 20 spaces that lead up to the duchess's. Invite them to decorate the game board with pictures of a snowy woods and the duchess's palace. (See the sample board game on the next page.) Have students each make or find a game piece.

2 Give each group ten or more 3-by-5-inch unlined index cards. Explain that these are Problem Cards. Each child in the group should take two cards and write down a new problem Irene could face on her journey. Help children brainstorm problems. Point out that the problem can be realistic, such as being hungry or getting lost, or the problem could be more fantasy oriented, such as meeting a tricky talking animal. (Note: If they haven't already done so, invite children to think of new story problems by filling in the reproducible on page 38.)

3 To make the game more exciting, have children randomly label each Problem Card with a number from one to five. That number will be the number of spaces they can move their piece up the board after thinking of a solution to the problem.

4 To play the game, children should pick a Problem Card. After reading the problem aloud, the child has to think of a possible solution. Once the child has "solved" the problem, he or she can move their Irene piece toward the duchess's the number of spaces indicated on the card. The first player to reach the duchess's wins.

Sample Board Game

Other Books to Use with This Activity

Chester the Worldly Pig by Bill Peet (Houghton Mifflin, 1968)

Look Out, Patrick! By Paul Gerghaty (Macmillan, 1990)

Tom Thumb by Richard Jesse Watson (Harcourt Brace, 1989)

Best Friends

by Miriam Cohen (SIMON & SCHUSTER, 1973)

At the beginning of the school day, Jim and Paul are best friends. Then a series of misunderstandings leads them to become almost enemies. How Jim and Paul solve their problem makes for a satisfying ending with which children will easily identify. This simple, realistic story will help children understand how plots can come from the problems they face in everyday life.

Learning Goals

* Explore a story problem that comes from everyday life.

* Map a story plot that comes from children's own problems and experiences.

Before Reading the Book

Tell the class that they are about to read a story about two friends at school who have a problem. Explain that their problem is the kind that might happen to any child in their class on any day. Invite children to brainstorm a list of problems that might happen to friends at school. Talk about how some of these problems could be made into a story.

While Reading the Book

As you read, invite children to discuss how Jim is feeling after each new episode. Encourage them to predict how he and Paul might solve their problem.

After Reading the Book

Invite children to share their reactions to the story. Ask them to describe the story problem. Why do they think Jim and Paul became almost enemies? Do they think the problem was Jim's fault? Paul's fault? neither or both boys' fault? Help children to understand that although the events in the classroom contributed to the boys' problem, the way each boy felt about the events was more important than the events themselves. Then invite children to discuss the ending. Ask why they think saving the chicks helped Jim and Paul become friends again. Invite children to suggest other ways Jim and Paul might have solved their problem.

Activity Page

The reproducible on page 42 invites children to summarize the story's problem and think of a new solution by writing advice letters to and from Jim.

Name _____

 # Advice Letters

How do you think Jim should solve his problem? On the first piece of stationery, write a letter from Jim describing the problem. On the next piece of stationery, help Jim think of a new way to make up with Paul.

Dear_____ (Write your name.)

_____

_____

_____

Signed, Jim

Dear Jim,

_____

_____

_____

Signed, _____ (Write your name.)

Teaching Story Elements With Favorite Books Scholastic Professional Books

Advice Box Stories

The plot of *Best Friends* centers on a completely believable series of incidents that happen to two children at school. This activity encourages children to recognize that their own lives can inspire story plots. First, children will write letters seeking advice for a problem. Then, the group will use the letters to brainstorm story maps.

Introducing the Activity

Invite children to share problems they have had with friends, at school, or at home. Then point out that the experiences and problems that ordinary children have every day can make excellent story plots.

Creating the Advice Letters and Answers

1 Show children a large box (such as one that boots come in) in which you have made a slit in the lid and labeled "Advice." Introduce the idea of an advice box by saying that people who have a problem sometimes write letters to an expert and the expert writes back telling them what to do. Tell children that this is the class advice box. Explain that they are going to think of problems that real children might have and then write about it in a letter for the advice box. Suggest that their problem can be real or one they make up. Before beginning, you may want to brainstorm kinds of everyday problems such as those below.

Problems Real Children Have

- breaking something valuable
- not being able to do something other children can do
- fighting with a friend, or with a sister or brother
- being afraid of something
- being lonely or bored

2 Have children write their letters and encourage them to add as many details about the problem as they can.

3 After each child has contributed a letter to the advice box, gather the class together. Choose letters to read aloud. Then ask children for their advice on how to solve the problem. Help children see how these problems and solutions might be made into story plots by filling out a story map such as the one on the next page. Remind children that even if these letters tell about a real child's problem, they can use their imaginations when they add the story details or think of resolutions. Children may want to write or act out one of their real-life problem stories.

Main Character
Rosita, a 7-year-old girl

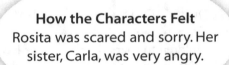

Character's Problem
Rosita broke her older sister's special doll.

How the Characters Felt
Rosita was scared and sorry. Her sister, Carla, was very angry.

Other Events or Details
Carla told Rosita never to play with her toys.

The Solution
Rosita saves all her money and buys Carla a new doll.

Other Books to Use with This Activity

A Chair for My Mother by Vera Williams (William Morrow, 1983)

Peter's Chair by Ezra Jack Keats (Harper & Row, 1967)

Timothy Goes to School by Rosemary Wells (Dial, 1981)

· S e t t i n g ·

To explore setting is to both look very closely at a book and to extend far beyond it to the world at large. It can mean focusing on something as particular as how an author describes a blade of grass, or it can inspire something as wide-ranging as the study of distant places and long-ago times. Some books are unimaginable without their settings. The *Little House* books without the prairie would be unrecognizable. Other books may appear to have barely any setting whatsoever. But however much attention the author focuses on the setting, it is always present and always affects everything else in the story.

The books in this section were chosen to provide many different ways of looking at setting. There are books that encourage children to engage with life in different times and places, such as *When I Was Young in the Mountains* or *The Day of Ahmed's Secret*. Other books, such as Jane Yolen's *Owl Moon*, help children focus on how authors describe natural settings, whereas Chris Van Allsburg's *The Polar Express* introduces fantasy settings. As you use the lessons that follow, keep these basic learning goals in mind.

✸ Help children to identify settings by looking for clues that tell them that a book is taking place now or long ago, in a place like their own or far away, or in the real world or in a fantasy world.

✸ Encourage children to use the information in literature to develop their understanding of new worlds, times, and places.

✸ Focus children's attention on how authors and illustrators use language and visual imagery to evoke a time, a place, and a mood.

✸ Ask children to use what they know about a book's setting to predict the kinds of people, events, or tone they will encounter.

✸ Note the changes of setting within a single book and how each setting helps to move the story forward.

Introducing Setting: A Setting Hunt

Explain to children that they are going to be studying setting—or where and when books take place. Invite children to go on a Setting Hunt. Ask them to each find a picture book from the classroom library that tells a story. Gather the class together and review the settings in each book. As you go through the pictures in the book, ask children: *Do you think this book takes place now? long ago? in the future? How can you tell?* Point out to children that clothing, buildings, and modes of transportation are often good indicators of where and when a story takes place. Invite children to notice whether the book seems to take place in the country or the city, in a place like their own or in some other part of the world. Since fantasy worlds are also an important kind of literary setting, ask children if they think the stories are about something that could really happen. Do they think there is magic in the book or characters that could never exist in the real world? As you go through the books, you may want to start a list of kinds of settings which you can add to as you continue your setting studies.

When I Was Young in the Mountains

by Cynthia Rylant

(DUTTON, 1982)

This poetic memoir lovingly recalls the author's girlhood in the Appalachian Mountains, when evening meals were cornbread and okra, the general store smelled of sweet butter, and children swam in the watering hole during long summer days. Detailed illustrations of rural life and the book's repetitive language structure will help children to focus on the many clues that describe a very particular time and place.

Learning Goals

✳ **Explore a setting by looking at how characters live their daily lives.**

✳ **Compare a book's world with children's own world.**

✳ **Create a literary setting using children's own time and place.**

Before Reading the Book

Invite children to share stories they have heard about growing up in the olden days. Ask: *How was life different then? What did children do for fun? What was school like? What inventions do we have now that didn't exist when your grandparents were young?* Explain that the book they are about to read takes place in the Appalachian Mountains at the time when their parents or grandparents were children. You may want to show them the area on a map.

While Reading the Book

To reinforce children's appreciation of the book's setting, stop every few pages to ask: *How is this the same as your world? How is it different?* Remind children that the illustrations often provide as much information about the setting as does the text.

After Reading the Book

After finishing the book, ask children if they would like to live in the book's world. In what ways would they enjoy it more than their own time and place? How would it be less enjoyable? What could they do in the book's world that they can't do in their own? What can they do in their world that the children in the book can't do? Did any details of the children's life surprise them?

You may want to go through the book and make a chart that compares and contrasts life in the book's world with life in the children's world. For example:

In the Mountains	In Our World
They pump water for their baths and heat it on the stove.	Hot water comes right to our bathtubs.

Activity Page

The reproducible on page 48 invites children to compare and contrast their homes with the author's childhood home in the mountains.

Name _____

House Tales

Pick a room in the book's world. Draw what you think it looked like. Then draw the same room in your world. On the lines below, write how your drawings are the same and how they are different.

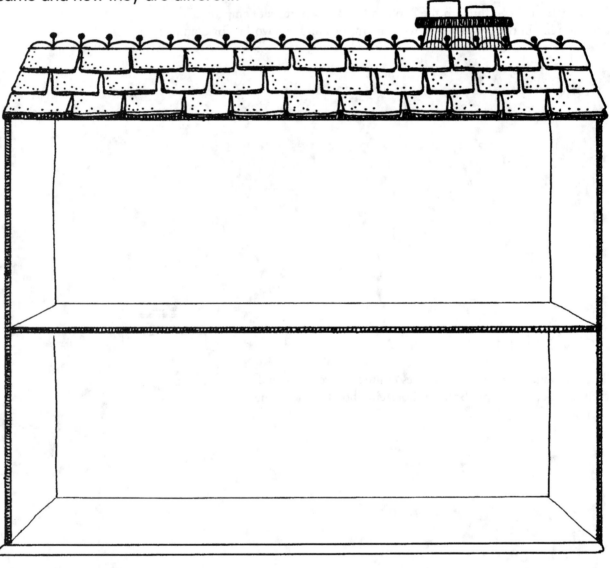

_____

_____

_____

Teaching Story Elements With Favorite Books Scholastic Professional Books

When We Were Young In... Class Book

When I Was Young in the Mountains creates its strong setting simply by describing how people lived every day in a particular time and place. The activity below invites children to create a class book about their own time and place. An alternate activity asks children to put together a book on life in the olden days by gathering experiences from their families and older people in the school and community.

Introducing the Activity

Invite children to write a class book about daily life in their own time and place based on *When I Was Young in the Mountains*. To get started, review the book and focus on the kinds of events and details the author chose to tell about her life in the mountains. Then brainstorm similar kinds of experiences about children's own lives. Some topics to consider include:

* **What we do in school**

* **Special ways we celebrate holidays**

* **Games we play**

* **Special events in the community or at school (picnics, parades, plays, etc.)**

* **Special times with our families**

* **Daily routines (favorite stories we read before going to bed, experiences walking to school)**

* **Favorite places in the community (what we do in the park, the store, etc.)**

* **Clothes we wear, books we read, TV shows we watch**

Making the Memories Book

Invite children to pick one or more of the memories they just talked about and to write it down. Encourage them to use the language pattern of the book: "When I was young in . . ." Remind children that the author of the book told not only what happened but also about how she felt, how a place looked or smelled, or what someone said. Encourage children to illustrate their memories and bind them into a class or individual book.

Life in the Olden Days

Older children may want to make a class book about life in the olden days. To begin, have children share family stories about their parents' or grandparents' childhoods. Then share stories yourself or invite other adults from the school or community for children to interview. If there is a senior citizen center or senior residence in your community, you may want to arrange a visit. After children have accumulated their anecdotes and memories, show pictures of what people looked like in the times they heard about. To make the book, invite children to choose one memory and write a few lines about it. Pick a common phrase such as *Long ago* or *When our parents were young...* to start each page. Have children illustrate their pages and bind them into a class book.

Other Books to Use with This Activity

The Chalk Doll by Charlotte Pomerantz (Lippincott, 1989)

On Granddaddy's Farm by Thomas B. Allen (Knopf, 1989)

Ox-Cart Man by Donald Hall (Puffin Books, 1983)

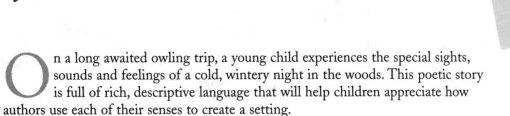

Owl Moon

by Jane Yolen (PHILOMEL, 1987)

On a long awaited owling trip, a young child experiences the special sights, sounds and feelings of a cold, wintery night in the woods. This poetic story is full of rich, descriptive language that will help children appreciate how authors use each of their senses to create a setting.

Learning Goals

❋ **Explore how an author describes a physical setting using her senses.**

❋ **Visualize a setting using the author's images.**

❋ **Describe a setting in children's own environment.**

Before Reading the Book

Invite children to share experiences of being outdoors at night. If possible, on the day before reading the book, ask children to go outside at night with an adult and jot down their observations. Ask: *How do you feel when you're outside at night? What special sounds can or did you hear? How do things look different?* Try to elicit nighttime sights, sounds, and feelings such as crickets, fireflies, shadows, the stars, or the damp ground. Ask how being outside at night seems different from being outside during the day. Tell children that the book they are about to read is about a child who walks through the woods on a cold winter night. Ask them to predict some of the things the child will feel, see, hear, and smell.

While Reading the Book

As you read, draw attention to the way the author describes the cold, quiet, and darkness of the night.

After Reading the Book

After reading the book, ask children if they would enjoy making an owling trip like the child in the book did. What part would they like the best? What would they like the least? Encourage children to use their own words to describe some the things the child saw, felt, and heard. Then ask: *What do you think the child enjoyed about the owling trip?* Try to guide children to understand that being outside at night was as important a part of the experience as seeing the owl.

Setting Poetry

In *Owl Moon*, Jane Yolen helps the reader feel the physical setting of a woods at night by paying close attention to what things looked, sounded, and felt like. In the first part of this activity, children create poetry based on the sensory descriptions of the setting in *Owl Moon*. Then they use their senses to write poems that describe a familiar setting such as the school playground.

Introducing the Activity

Together, look through *Owl Moon* for examples of what the child saw, heard, and felt while traveling through the woods. Point out that often the author describes not only the sights, sounds, and feelings but also tells something about what these things looked, sounded, and felt like. You may want to simply list students' responses on a chart such as the one shown below, then invite students to work together to write their own setting poems. They may also enjoy creating illustrations from collage materials, such as black, gray, and white tissue paper, to evoke the story's wintry, nighttime setting.

THE WOODS AT NIGHT

What They Saw	What the Things Looked Like
• trees	black and pointy, like giant statues
• snow	whiter than the milk in a cereal bowl

What They Heard	What the Things Sounded Like
• feet	crunching over the crisp snow
• train whistle	long and low, like a sad song

Making the Setting Poetry Mural

1 Tell children that they are going to visit a place in their school or community to collect sights, sounds, and feelings just as the child did in *Owl Moon*.

2 Take the class out to the school playground, a nearby park or pond, or some other setting with interesting sights and sounds. Give each child a copy of the Activity Page on page 54 and a clipboard. (If clipboards are not easily available, thin, hardcover books and large binder clips make a good substitute.) Ask children to notice, sketch, and write about what they see, hear, smell, and feel.

3 Back in the classroom, have children share their observations and list them on a chart. Then invite the class to create a large setting mural on craft paper. Assign individuals or groups of children to draw or paint one or two items on your list. You may want to have children work on the mural a few at a time.

4 After the mural is complete, hang it up and gather the class in a circle. Point to a picture on the mural. First, ask children to tell what it is. Then, ask them to describe it. Remind them to use words that describe colors, shapes, smells, and movements. Create a class poem by writing the name of the picture and the describing words on chart paper. Follow each new entry with the word *like* as shown below. Then encourage children to think of a comparison. For example, if you have written that the slide is shiny, ask children to think of something else that is shiny, such as stars at night or tin foil. Add these comparisons to your poem.

At the Playground
The silver slide shines like a star at night.
Children laugh and shout like crows screeching.
White *jump* ropes turn each second
like the hands of a clock.

Other Books to Use with This Activity

The Listening Walk by Paul Showers (Harper Trophy, 1993)

The Storm Book by Charlotte Zolotow (Harper Trophy, 1989)

Time of Wonder by Robert McCloskey (Viking, 1957)

Name _____

A Sense of Place

Collect sights, sounds, and feelings from a place you visit. Draw or write about them in the boxes below.

At the _____ (name of place)

I saw...

It looked like...

I heard...

It sounded like...

I felt...

It felt like...

Teaching Story Elements With Favorite Books   Scholastic Professional Books

The Day of Ahmed's Secret

by Florence Parry Heide and Judith Heide Gilliland (Lᴏᴛʜʀᴏᴘ, Lᴇᴇ ᴀɴᴅ Sʜᴇᴘᴀʀᴅ, 1990)

Ahmed has learned to write his name. But before he can show his family, he travels on his donkey cart through the busy streets of modern Cairo. Ancient market stalls, camel caravans, and traffic jams are just a few of the sights, sounds, and scenes that will acquaint children with this faraway part of the world. Exploring *The Day of Ahmed's Secret* will encourage children to use a work of literature to find out about a culture that is different from their own.

Learning Goals

✳ **Use text and illustrations to learn about life in unfamiliar settings.**

✳ **Create artifacts that tell about life in the book's world.**

✳ **Compare and contrast the book's world with children's own.**

Before Reading the Book

Ask children to describe what they see and hear when walking through the center of their city or town. Encourage them to name kinds of stores, public buildings, and vehicles. If children in your class come from different parts of the world, invite them to share how your community differs from the town or city they come from. Tell children that the book they are about to read is about a boy who travels through the city of Cairo on a donkey cart. Explain that Cairo is a large city in the country of Egypt. Point to Egypt on a world map. Indicate the desert surrounding Cairo. Have children share what they know about Egypt. Invite them to predict some things Ahmed might see on his journey.

While Reading the Book

As you read, stop every few pages and have children discuss the people, buildings, and activities they see in the illustrations. Invite them to guess Ahmed's secret.

Name _____

What Did Ahmed See?

What did Ahmed see while riding on his donkey cart? Fill in the box below with buildings, people, and other things that Ahmed passed on his journey.

Teaching Story Elements With Favorite Books   Scholastic Professional Books

After Reading the Book

After reading the book, ask children what surprised them about the city of Cairo. Encourage children to observe that Cairo is a much older city than any in the United States and that many of the places Ahmed passes could be a thousand years old. Then point out that while many aspects of life in Cairo are different from life in the children's own town or city, there are also things that are the same. Invite children to find and name sights in the book that they might also find at home.

Activity Page

The reproducible on page 56 will help children appreciate how much they can learn about a faraway place from a book by drawing a scene from Ahmed's journey.

Place Capsules

Through reading *The Day of Ahmed's Secret*, children will become familiar with many things that are part of the daily life of a modern Egyptian child. The following activity will encourage children to compare and contrast their daily lives with Ahmed's by creating two "place capsules." The first will include objects that tell about Ahmed's life, and the second will tell about their own lives.

Introducing the Activity

Introduce children to the idea of a time capsule. Explain that people make time capsules by filling containers with objects from their daily lives, such as clothes, books, tools, newspapers, or toys. Then they bury the containers hoping that future generations will be able to learn about their culture by studying the capsule's contents. Tell children that they are going to make place capsules, which are like time capsules except that they try to tell about life in a particular place. Explain that they will be making a place capsule about Ahmed's life and one about their own lives.

Reviewing the Setting

Before sending children off to make their place capsules, review some of the things they can find out about life in Cairo by reading *The Day of Ahmed's Secret*. You may want to go through the book and brainstorm a list of objects that they can make, find, draw, or cut out to include in their capsules. Use the list on the next page to help children come up with possibilities. You may also wish to provide picture reference books about life in Egypt for children to look at. *Cairo* by R. Conrad Stein (Children's Press, 1996) is a good one.

THINGS IN AHMED'S WORLD

* decorated cloth as shown in the book

* hats, sandals, and other articles of clothing

* jugs for storing water

* baskets for carrying things

* Ahmed's donkey and donkey cart

* camels and/or their decorative bridles and cloths

* rosewater bottles

* rice and beans

* mosaic plates like the one in Ahmed's home

Creating the Place Capsules

1 Give children shoe boxes to decorate and use as place capsules.

2 Set out pieces of cloth, yarn, cardboard, paper-towel tubes, clay, empty plastic bottles, craft sticks, and other materials for creating objects. If children cannot make certain objects, let them draw pictures of them and cut them out.

3 After children have made Ahmed's place capsule, let them make a similar one about their lives. Suggest that they include items that correspond to the ones they included in Ahmed's capsule. For example, if they made or drew an Egyptian hat, they may want to make a hat they would wear; or if they included Ahmed's donkey cart, they may want to include a bicycle.

4 Invite children to share their capsules with classmates and to talk about the contents of each.

Other Books to Use with This Activity

Our Home Is the Sea by Riki Levinson (Dutton, 1988)

Tonight Is Carnaval by Arthur Dorros (Dutton, 1991)

Tree of Cranes by Alan Say (Houghton Mifflin, 1991)

The Polar Express

by Chris Van Allsburg (HOUGHTON MIFFLIN, 1985)

On Christmas Eve, a mysterious train appears outside a boy's home and takes him to the North Pole to receive the first gift of Christmas. This dreamlike story invites children to enter a richly imagined fantasy world and to consider the features that help to make a fantasy setting.

Learning Goals

* **Explore the elements that make up a fantasy world.**
* **Note changes of setting within a story.**
* **Create new fantasy worlds using the book as a model.**

Before Reading the Book

Tell children that they are going to read a story about a boy who goes to an imaginary place. Ask children if they have ever wanted to go to an imaginary place. Invite them to describe what their imaginary place would be like. What kind of people or creatures would live there? What would the houses and buildings look like? How would they get there? Show children the cover of the book and read the title. Give children small pieces of paper and ask them to draw one thing they think they will see in the story.

While Reading the Book

As you read, encourage children to note when and how the book's setting changes from the real world to fantasy.

After Reading the Book

Ask children what they thought of the story. Do they think what happened was real? Or was it all the boy's dream? Talk about the fantasy elements in the story. Ask children to identify parts of the story that could happen in the ordinary world. Which parts would probably never happen in real life? (If children believe in Santa Claus, you can explain that while he may exist, no one has ever seen him or where he lives so that the world in the story still comes from the author's imagination.) Encourage children to notice that even when the boy is in the fantasy world, many of the elements, such as the way the train looked or the buildings in Santa's city, were almost like real life. Point out that fantasy worlds often combine elements from the real world and elements from the author's imagination.

Name _____

Real and Fantasy

Which things in <u>The Polar Express</u> could you see or do in real life? Which parts of the story are fantasy? In each box below, draw or write about something that was real and something that was fantasy.

On the Train Ride:

Real

Fantasy

At the North Pole:

Real

Fantasy

Teaching Story Elements With Favorite Books Scholastic Professional Books

To help children begin thinking about their own fantasy worlds, ask if they would like to take a train ride like the boy's. What special features would the train have? Where would the train go?

Activity Page

The reproducible on page 60 will reinforce children's understanding of fantasy versus reality by having them draw or write about real and fantasy elements from settings in the book.

Fantasy World Trading Cards

*T*he *Polar Express* contains many elements common to literary fantasy worlds, such as magical transportation, creatures who do special things, and an unworldly place. This activity encourages children to create their own ideas for a fantasy world by making trading cards that show the world's creatures, vehicles, and other features.

Introducing the Activity

Invite them to think about a fantasy world they would like to visit. To help organize their thinking, you may want to ask some of the following questions and list sample responses:

Who Lives in My Fantasy World?

What do they look like?

How do they talk?

What are their special powers?

What do they do all day?

What are they called?

What Is My Fantasy World Like?

What is it called?

What does it look like?

Where do the inhabitants live?

What kind of magical places/objects are there?

How Can I Get to My Fantasy World?

By magical vehicles?

By making a wish?

By a secret passageway?

Making the Trading Cards

1 Give each child five to ten blank, unlined index cards. Explain to the class that they will use these cards to draw and write about their fantasy world. Point out that trading cards generally have a picture on one side and information about the picture on the other. It might be helpful to show examples of baseball or other trading cards.

2 Tell children that at least one card should show a picture of the fantasy world and tell its name. Other cards can tell about the characters who live in the world, or about magical vehicles or objects, or can show special places in the world and tell what happens there.

3 After they have finished, invite each child to show their trading cards and talk about the world they have created. In their free time, children may want to mix and match cards to see how their fantasy worlds combine, or use their cards as story starters.

Other Books to Use with This Activity

Hey, Al by Arthur Yorinks (Farrar, Straus & Giroux, 1986)

My Father's Dragon by Ruth S. Gannet (Knopf, 1987)

Where the Wild Things Are by Maurice Sendak (Harper & Row, 1963)

· T h e m e ·

Exploring theme can be the most personal and rewarding way of engaging with a work of literature. Children's stories are traditionally rich with strong themes. Classic tales such as "Cinderella," "The Ugly Duckling," or "The Three Little Pigs" have inspired generations of children to believe in the powers of kindness, hard work, tolerance, and other virtues. The messages in these stories are far from lost on children and their enduring popularity suggests how deeply they care about such themes.

Teachers of younger children sometimes feel that the concept of theme is too abstract or difficult to introduce in a meaningful way. However, there are many simple methods of helping even the youngest children discuss and work with a story's theme. Considering what characters learned, the decisions they made, and why they are rewarded or punished are often easy entry points for theme discussions. Activities in which children extend a story's theme to their own lives help to reinforce their understanding and encourage them to connect with literature on a deeper level.

Fairy tales, fables, and other classic literature are ideal for introducing the story element of theme. Often these stories present a strong message in a clear and concise way. The books in this section include old favorites such as *The Ugly Duckling*, as well as contemporary stories grounded in the folk tradition, such as William Steig's *Amos & Boris*, and John Steptoe's *Mufaro's Beautiful Daughters*. The fourth book, *Brother Eagle, Sister Sky*, invites children to explore a different kind of message—about taking care of the earth. The discussions and activities that accompany these books introduce children to the following basic understandings about story themes:

* Stories often contain messages about what is important in life; about how we can deal with our problems; or about how we can feel, act, and be better. These messages are called themes.

* Themes are usually expressed through what happens to characters during the story. Sometimes we can discover these themes by looking at what the characters learn or how they change and grow.

* Even though stories may be about characters who are very different from us, we can apply their experiences to our own lives and learn from them.

Theme is the most personal literary element. It asks readers to consider what the story means to them and to relate that message to their own lives. After you discuss the stories, give children time to express the meaning in their own words and tell how that message might be important to them.

The Ugly Duckling

A Tale from Hans Christian Andersen, retold by Lorinda Bryan Cauley

(HARCOURT BRACE, 1979)

This moving tale about the despised Ugly Duckling who grows into a beautiful swan offers a simple theme with which children can identify emotionally. By relating the duckling's feelings to their own, children will have the opportunity to consider how stories can help them learn and grow.

Learning Goals

✳ **Identify a simple theme by exploring what a character learned.**

✳ **Relate a theme to children's own experiences.**

Introducing the Book

Tell children that they are going to read a story about a character who is very different from everyone around him. Invite children to tell about times they have felt different from those around them. Ask them to tell how being different made them feel. Encourage children to suggest ways that being different might be a good thing.

While Reading the Book

As you read the book, invite children to talk about the duckling's feelings and to share their reactions to the other ducks' behavior. Ask what they would say to the Ugly Duckling to make him feel better. What would they say to the other ducks?

After Reading the Book

Ask children what they thought of the story. What did they feel about the way the duckling was treated? Did they think the Ugly Duckling was really ugly? What would be another way to describe him? *(different from the rest)* How did they feel when the Ugly Duckling became a swan? Was that a good way to end the story? Why or why not?

Encourage children to extend the theme of the story to their own lives by asking why they think the author wanted to tell this story. What could people learn by reading *The Ugly Duckling*? How might it help them feel better about themselves or behave differently towards others? Try to elicit that even though the story is about being considered ugly, the message might apply to anyone who is different in any way and feels bad about it. Invite children to share times when they have felt bad about being different. Ask how they could think of themselves as "swans" during those times.

Activity

The reproducible on page 66 invites children to reflect on the story's theme by writing a message to the Ugly Duckling and a message to the other ducks.

Cooperative Theme Trees

This activity invites children to contribute "leaves" to bulletin board trees by drawing and writing about a story's meaning and how it relates to their own experiences. Books that inspire children to identify with the plight of the main character, such as the Ugly Duckling, are ideal for this group activity that highlights how literature helps each of us to grow in our own personal ways.

Getting Ready

Cut out of construction or craft paper two large paper tree trunks with branches. Attach the trees to a bulletin board. Leave plenty of room on each side for children to add drawings and writing to the branches. You may also want to cut out large leaf shapes from paper for children to write and draw on. Label the display "Our Ugly Duckling Theme Trees."

Introducing the Activity

Share with children that the messages in stories can help us grow and become stronger inside. Explain that what a character experiences in a story can be similar to what we experience and that what a character learns can help us to learn too. Indicate the bulletin board trees. Suggest that leaves are a sign that a tree is growing. Tell children that the leaves on these trees will show ways the Ugly Duckling grew inside. The leaves will also show ways that reading *The Ugly Duckling* helped children feel stronger and grow too.

Name _____

Help the Ugly Duckling

Can you help the Ugly Duckling? On the first sheet of paper, write a message that will make the Ugly Duckling feel better. On the second sheet of paper, tell the other ducks what you think about how they acted.

Dear Ugly Duckling,

_____

_____

_____

_____

_____

_____

Dear other ducks,

_____

_____

_____

_____

_____

_____

Teaching Story Elements With Favorite Books   Scholastic Professional Books

Making the Theme Trees

1 Give children each one or two plain or leaf-shaped pieces of construction paper and ask them to write one or two sentences telling what the Ugly Duckling or the other characters learned in the story. Invite children to illustrate their sentences on the same or a different leaf.

2 Attach the leaves to one of the theme trees. Together, read what each leaf says. Then remind children that characters aren't the only ones who learn in stories. Readers can grow and learn things, too. Point to the second tree and tell children that this tree is for showing how each child in the class can learn something different from *The Ugly Duckling*.

3 To help children organize their thoughts, ask some of the following questions: *Have you ever felt different like the Ugly Duckling, or not as good as others? How might reading the story help you to feel better?* Ask children to think of themselves as swans during those times. Some children may choose to focus on the role of the other ducks and on the message of tolerance. Ask: *Have you ever seen anyone act like the other ducks by making fun of someone who was different? How did you feel during those times? How might reading the story help these people to change their attitudes or help you to speak up to them?* Encourage children to use specific examples from their own lives as they make their second leaf.

4 When each child has contributed a leaf, invite children to read and elaborate on their contributions.

It's wrong to be mean to people because they are different. The Ugly Duckling was nice and he became a swan. The other ducklings just became ducks.
—Tamika

I speak Korean. That makes me different like the Ugly Duckling. But I know two languages. That way I'm like a swan.
—Myung

Once everyone else was swimming but me. I felt like the Ugly Duckling because I was afraid.
—Jorge

Other Books to Use with This Activity

Crow Boy by Taro Yashima (Viking, 1955; Puffin Books, 1976)

Frederick by Leo Lionni (Knopf, 1967)

Leo the Late Bloomer by Robert Kraus (Crowell, 1971)

No Good in Art by Miriam Cohen (Greenwillow, 1980)

Amos & Boris

by William Steig

(FARRAR, STRAUS & GIROUX, 1971)

C an a tiny mouse and a giant whale become best friends? Amos and Boris find a way in this humorous and touching story about a highly unlikely pair of animal friends. Based on Aesop's "The Lion and the Mouse," *Amos & Boris* presents a simple message about the power of good works and friendship that children will care about and relate to their own lives.

Learning Goals

* Identify a simple story theme.
* Pick out story details that reveal and express the theme.
* Innovate new story situations using the same theme.

Before Reading the Book

Ask children to draw a picture of themselves and a good friend. Beneath their pictures, have them write two ways that they and their friend are alike. Then ask them to write two ways that they are different. As children share their work, encourage them to discuss how friends can appear different but still have many common interests and feelings. Then tell children that they are going to read about a mouse and whale who become good friends. Ask them to think of ways an imaginary mouse and whale could have fun together.

While Reading the Book

As you read, have children notice Amos's and Boris's differences and how they manage to overcome them. Invite children to predict if and how Amos will return Boris's good deed.

After Reading the Book

Invite children to share their reactions to the story. Ask if they were surprised that Amos and Boris became friends. Encourage them to explain why Amos and Boris made such good friends and to describe why their friendship was unusual. Then give children the opportunity to "discover" the story's theme by asking what they can learn about being good friends from reading *Amos & Boris*. As you discuss the question, focus on some or all of the following ideas about friendship:

* **It is possible to become friends with someone very different from you.**

* **It is important to look past surface differences to find the things we have in common.**

* **Helping someone is a good thing, even if you don't think they will ever be able to help you back.**

Encourage children to appreciate the subtleties in this last theme by saying: *Boris helped Amos, even though he thought Amos would never be able to help him in return. How does that make it a better story about true friendship?*

After children have shared their thoughts, ask them to each write a sentence or two telling what they learned about friendship from reading *Amos & Boris*. Have children share their sentences.

Activity Page

The reproducible on page 70 will help reinforce the theme of *Amos & Boris* by inviting children to create new animal friends who are very different from one another. (Note: Children creating individual Same-Message Stories may want to use this page as a prewriting organizer. See page 71.)

Name _____

Friends Can Be Very Different

Amos and Boris became good friends, even though they were very different. Draw two other animals who are very different. Then write about how they could be friends.

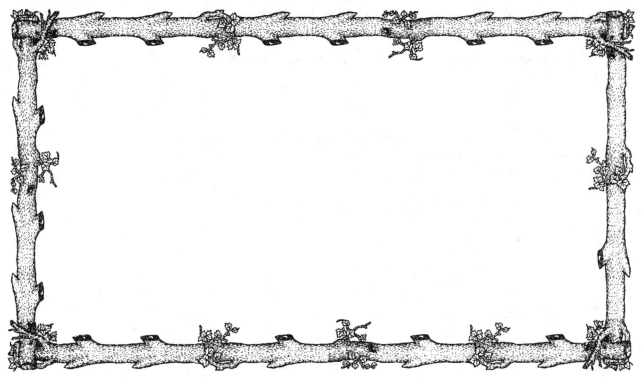

Tell how your two animals could have fun together.

_____

_____

Tell how your two animals could help each other.

_____

_____

Teaching Story Elements With Favorite Books   Scholastic Professional Books

Same-Message Stories

Picking out those story details that relate to the author's message is an important skill to develop when exploring theme. This activity invites children to create a new story using the theme of differences and friendship found in *Amos & Boris*. By changing the animal characters and how they enjoy each other's company, children will clarify their understanding of how the story's theme differs from plot, character, and other story elements.

Introducing the Activity

Review with children the theme of differences and friendship found in *Amos & Boris*. Point out that it is possible to make up a story with the same message but with new story details. Explain that the theme can be expressed using new animal characters who meet and become friends. These new characters will suggest different ways of having fun together and even different ways of helping each other. In other words, the story details will change but the message of the story will remain the same.

Writing the Same-Message Class Book

1 With younger students, invite volunteers to suggest two new animals who are quite different from each other. One might be big and the other little, as in *Amos & Boris*; or one might live underground and the other in the water. Write these animal names on the chalkboard—for example, Eagle and Frog.

2 Have children brainstorm three ways that these animals are different. For example: An eagle flies; a frog hops. An eagle lives in a tree; a frog lives in a pond. An eagle has claws on its feet; a frog has webbed feet.

3 Next, ask children to suggest things that these two animals might have in common or enjoy doing together. Point out that these could be activities that only fantasy animals might do, such as reading stories together or playing hide-and-seek; or they could be based on the animals' real characteristics. For example, the eagle might take the frog flying.

4 Ask children to suggest ways each animal might help the other. For example, the frog could find something that the eagle dropped into the water.

5 Once you have decided on your pair of new animal friends, use your list of their differences to write a brief introduction to a class book. For example:

> One day an eagle named Juan met a frog named Akimi.
> "We are so different," thought Juan. "I fly and Akimi hops.
> I live in a tree and Akimi lives in the water. I am big and
> Akimi is small. We will never be friends."

6 Hand out large sheets of construction paper or tagboard and let each child create one or more class book pages showing the animal pair having fun or helping each other. Have children begin their contribution with the phrase *But even though they are different…* and describe how the characters might help each other or have fun together. Let several children work together to create a cover and then punch holes in the left side of the pages and bind them with yarn or "O" rings. Read the book together and discuss its message. Discuss how it compares to the message of *Amos & Boris*.

7 Older children may prefer to make up their own same-message stories using original characters. Follow steps 1 to 4 above to help children brainstorm ideas; or children may use the reproducible on page 70 to create their own animal characters and tell how these characters will have fun together and help each other. Encourage children to follow the simple structure of *Amos & Boris* as they write their stories. Invite them to illustrate their stories as well.

> But even though they are different they both like to eat pancakes. Nina
> BUT EVEN THOUGH THEY ARE DIFFERENT THEY BOTH LIKE TO WEAR HATS. JASAAN

Other Books to Use with This Activity

The Lion & the Mouse by Aesop (Troll, 1981)

Stellaluna by Janell Cannon (Harcourt Brace, 1993)

Swimmy by Leo Lionni (Knopf, 1963)

Brother Eagle, Sister Sky: A Message from Chief Seattle

(DIAL, 1991)

Based on a speech given by a great Native American chief more than 100 years ago, this poetic book makes an eloquent plea for loving and caring for the earth. By applying Chief Seattle's words to the world they live in, children will come to recognize how a book's message can change the way we think about an issue and inspire us to make the world a better place.

Learning Goals

* **Explore a theme that addresses a problem in the world.**

* **Recognize how a book's message can help change the way we act and think.**

* **Share an important message with others.**

Before Reading the Book

Tell children that the words in the book they are about to read were spoken by a real Native American chief over 100 years ago. Explain that Chief Seattle spoke these words to the people who forced the Native Americans to sell them their land. Tell children that the words express how Chief Seattle and his people feel about treating the earth and all of its plants and creatures. Invite children to share some of their feelings about how people should treat the earth, animals, and other living things.

While Reading the Book

As you read the story, pause to help children appreciate the poetic language Chief Seattle uses to describe the natural world. Ask why they think he talks about the earth and its creatures as family members. How is the earth like our family?

After Reading the Book

Invite children to share their reactions to the book. Have them describe in their own words how Chief Seattle feels about the earth. What does he say to show that the earth is very important to him? Then help children appreciate how Chief Seattle's message might affect people's actions. Ask: *How would you treat a river if you thought of it as your brother? How would you treat a flower if you thought of it as your sister? What*

Name _____

Speech! Speech!

Chief Seattle wrote the words in this book as a speech.
Make notes for your own speech about taking care of the earth.
Then practice your speech and deliver it to the class.

I love nature because

_____

_____

I feel sad when I see people hurting nature because

_____

_____

I think everyone should

_____

_____

That way we will all help the earth!

Teaching Story Elements With Favorite Books Scholastic Professional Books

does Chief Seattle mean when he says, "How can you buy the sky? How can you own the rain and the winds?" Have children share how they feel about Chief Seattle's message.

Activity Page

The reproducible on page 74 invites children to prepare a short speech based on the message of *Brother Eagle, Sister Sky*.

Spread the Message Take-Action Posters

Recognizing that books can speak about the problems of the world and encourage people to make the world a better place is an important dimension of exploring theme. This activity invites children to use a book's message to help improve the world by creating Take-Action Posters that share Chief Seattle's views.

Introducing the Activity

Point out that when Chief Seattle wrote the words in this book, it was over 100 years ago. Ask children how they think the world was different 100 years ago. Explain that when Chief Seattle was alive the world was less polluted than it is now and there were fewer buildings and cities and more forests and wild land. Ask children how they think Chief Seattle would feel about the pollution in the world today. How would he feel about all the land being built on? Tell children that they will be using Chief Seattle's words to make posters that encourage others to take care of the earth.

Making the Take-Action Posters

1 Invite children to work alone or in small groups to make their posters. Help them plan their posters by suggesting that they include some or all of the elements listed on the next page.

* a line or short passage from the book that describes Chief Seattle's feelings about the earth (For example, "You must give the rivers the kindness you would give to any brother.")

* a drawing that illustrates the passage and shows Chief Seattle's ideal world

* a drawing that shows the opposite of what Chief Seattle would like (for example, a river with pollution and litter)

* a statement or slogan that children make up telling how to improve the situation (For example, "Keep our rivers clean so we can drink and swim.")

Suggest that children make up a title for their posters, such as "A Message from Chief Seattle."

2 After children have completed their posters, discuss where they could hang them so they will do the most good. Possibilities include a hallway in the school, in the school or public library, in the post office, or in the windows of local businesses. If possible, arrange to display their posters at one or more of these locations and invite children to share their views and work with community members.

Other Books to Use with This Activity

And Still the Turtle Watched by Sheila MacGill-Callahan (Puffin Books, 1996)

The Great Kapok Tree by Lynn Cherry (Harcourt Brace, 1990)

The Lorax by Dr. Seuss (Random House, 1971)

Mufaro's Beautiful Daughters

by John Steptoe (LOTHROP, LEE & SHEPARD, 1987)

When a great king sends word throughout the kingdom that he is looking for a wife, Mufaro decides to send both of his daughters. But who will win the king's heart? The selfish and proud Manyara or the kind and loving Nyasha? Based on an African tale, this enthralling story offers a powerful message about the value of kindness and goodness.

Learning Goals

* ✳ **Recognize that authors express what they value through a story theme.**

* ✳ **Explore how characters' actions and choices reveal a theme.**

* ✳ **Relate the values of a story to children's own beliefs.**

Before Reading the Book

Tell children that they are going to read a story about a good king who is looking for a wife to help rule the land. Ask children what kind of person the king should look for. Together, make a list of qualities children think are important for a queen to have. As you review your list, ask children how the king might be able to tell if his future queen has those qualities.

While Reading the Book

As you read the story, invite children to note and describe the differences between the two sisters. Which sister do they hope will become queen? Do they think the king will be able to tell which is the good sister? How will he do that?

After Reading the Book

Ask children how they felt about the end of the book. Were they surprised when they found out that the garden snake was really the king? Why do they think the king turned himself into a snake? What did he hope to learn about Nyasha and Manyara that way? Invite children to describe how the two sisters acted on their way to the king's city. How do they think the way each sister acted showed the kind of person she was inside?

Finally, have children tell what they think is the message of the story. Ask: *What did the author say about what is important and what it means to be a good person?* Have children share why they think it is an important message.

Activity Page

The reproducible on page 78 will extend children's understanding of the story's message by inviting them to describe the kind of person they feel should become queen.

Name _____

A Queen Should Be...

Nyasha became queen because she was kind and good. What kind of person do you think should become queen? Pick two words from the list that describe your queen. Then tell how your queen would act that way.

kind

My queen is _____.

She _____.

honest

My queen is _____.

She _____.

Now draw a picture of your queen.

brave

strong

gentle

hardworking

Teaching Story Elements With Favorite Books Scholastic Professional Books

What We Value: Theme Ideas and Project Menu

Like many classic children's books, *Mufaro's Beautiful Daughters* offers a strong message about the value of being a good person. This activity invites the class to create a list of values and beliefs found in the story. By adding their own values and beliefs to the list, children will recognize that they too can create ideas for story themes. The follow-up activity menu gives children options for using their theme ideas to create theme bulletin board displays, theme skits, or theme banners.

Introducing the Activity

Point out that the author of *Mufaro's Beautiful Daughters* shared what he believes it means to be a good person through his story. Explain that, like *Mufaro's Beautiful Daughters*, many story themes come from what the author thinks it means to be good. Tell children that they will be developing their own ideas for story themes by discussing the qualities they feel make a good person.

Brainstorming Theme Ideas

Discuss with children why Nyasha becomes queen. Remind them of how she acted in the story. You may say, for example: *Nyasha was nice to the garden snake and the old woman*. Suggest that this gesture makes her a kind person. She also gave her food to the hungry boy. Suggest that this makes her generous. Begin a list such as the one below, using the theme ideas found in the story. Then invite children to add to the list by naming qualities that they think are important for a kind and good person to have. If children name qualities such as being good at sports or being smart, try to focus them on qualities that makes a person good inside or nice to others.

What We Value

It is important to be kind to others.
It is important to be generous and to share.
It is important to be honest.
It is important to work hard and not be lazy.
It is important to help others.
It is important to obey your parents and teachers.
It is important not to be cruel to animals.

Theme Idea Project Menu

Choose one of the following projects to help children put their theme ideas into action. Activity 1 is recommended for younger children. Activities 2 and 3 can be done with older children.

Activity 1: Theme Idea Bulletin Board

Invite children to pick a "value" from the list and draw and write about a time that they acted in that way. As you hang their work on a bulletin board, categorize them by theme labels such as "Kindness," "Honesty," etc. After the display is complete, go through each category. Have children discuss their pictures and think of possible story ideas for the theme category.

Activity 2: Theme Idea Skits

Invite children to pick a theme idea from the list and to create a skit that expresses it. They can create a skit from their own experiences by enacting a time that they acted kind or helpful or honest; or they may want to add a scene to *Mufaro's Beautiful Daughters* by making up a skit that shows how Nyasha loves animals or obeys her father, or one that shows Manyara behaving in the opposite way.

Activity 3: Theme Idea Banner

This activity invites small groups of children to choose a theme idea from the list and to work together to create a banner that expresses that idea. You may want to write the following list on the chalkboard to help get children started:

* **Draw and write about a time you acted in that way.**

* **Draw and write about a time you *didn't* act in that way.**

* **Write suggestions about how people can be more (kind, helpful, etc.).**

* **Draw pictures showing characters in books you have read acting in that way.**

* **Write about why you think being (kind, honest, etc.) is important.**

Other Books to Use with This Activity

The Empty Pot by Demi (Henry Holt, 1990)

The King's Equal by Katherine Paterson (HarperCollins, 1992)

The Story of Jumping Mouse by John Steptoe (William Morrow, 1984)